THE
TEACHER
50

Other ASCD books by Baruti K. Kafele

The Principal 50: Critical Leadership Questions for Inspiring Schoolwide Excellence

Closing the Attitude Gap: How to Fire Up Your Students to Strive for Success

Motivating Black Males to Achieve in School and in Life

THE TEACHER

50

Critical
Questions *for*
**Inspiring
Classroom
Excellence**

BARUTI K. KAFELE

Alexandria, Virginia USA

1703 N. Beauregard St. • Alexandria, VA 22311-1714 USA
Phone: 800-933-2723 or 703-578-9600 • Fax: 703-575-5400
Website: www.ascd.org • E-mail: member@ascd.org
Author guidelines: www.ascd.org/write

Deborah S. Delisle, *Executive Director;* Robert D. Clouse, *Managing Director, Digital Content &
Publications;* Stefani Roth, *Publisher;* Genny Ostertag, *Director, Content Acquisitions;* Julie Houtz,
Director, Book Editing & Production; Darcie Russell, *Editor;* Donald Ely, *Senior Graphic Designer;*
Mike Kalyan, *Manager, Production Services;* Cynthia Stock, *Typesetter;* Kyle Steichen, *Senior
Production Specialist*

PAPERBACK ISBN: 978-1-4166-2273-4   ASCD product #117009   n8/16
PDF E-BOOK ISBN: 978-1-4166-2275-8; see Books in Print for other formats.

Quantity discounts: 10–49, 10%; 50+, 15%; 1,000+, special discounts (e-mail programteam@
ascd.org or call 800-933-2723, ext. 5773, or 703-575-5773).
For desk copies, go to www.ascd.org/deskcopy.

Library of Congress Cataloging-in-Publication Data

Names: Kafele, Baruti K., author.
Title: The teacher 50 : critical questions for inspiring classroom excellence
  / Baruti K. Kafele.
Other titles: Teacher fifty
Description: Alexandria, Virginia : ASCD, 2016. | Includes bibliographical
  references and index.
Identifiers: LCCN 2016021779 (print) | LCCN 2016030717 (ebook) | ISBN
  9781416622734 (pbk.) | ISBN 9781416622758 (PDF)
Subjects: LCSH: Effective teaching. | Classroom environment.
Classification: LCC LB1025.3 .K35 2016 (print) | LCC LB1025.3 (ebook) | DDC
  371.102—dc23
LC record available at https://lccn.loc.gov/2016021779

30 29 28 27 26 25 24 23 22 21   6 7 8 9 10 11 12

To the teachers who read this book: In this age of criticizing, blaming, scrutinizing, and bashing teachers, I want to remind you all that YOU make the difference in students' lives. Your students will soar as high as you take them. Stay encouraged and stay inspired. YOU MATTER!

THE TEACHER 50

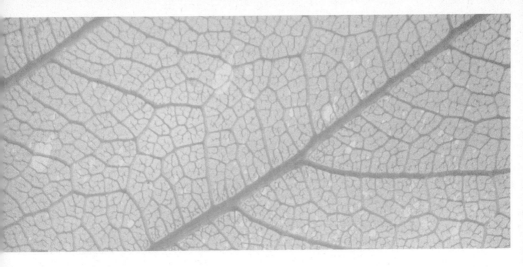

# INTRODUCTION

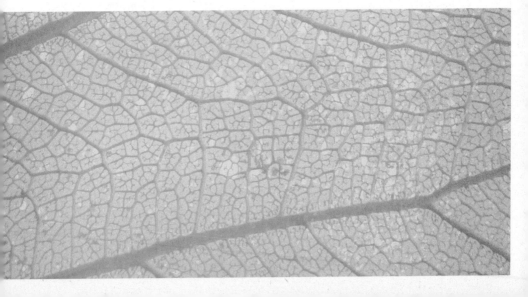

E ver since I entered the ranks of teaching in 1988 as a 5th grade teacher in Brooklyn, New York, the word *dream* has been a major part of my lexicon. For years, I would tell my students that they must dare to dream and they must dream big. This made perfectly good sense to me. After all, how can we expect youngsters to strive for excellence if they don't have a dream of excellence first? In addition to dreaming, I liked to encourage students to *imagine*—to imagine excellence, to imagine greatness, to imagine doing extraordinary things with the education they are receiving.

Several years into my teaching career, it occurred to me that my encouragements were probably falling on deaf ears. I concluded that I was speaking to students in a language that they didn't understand. The overwhelming majority of my students had grown up in economically disadvantaged communities where opportunities for success were grossly limited. How could they dream of or imagine a successful life when poverty was all around them?

When my students did dare to dream big, their dreams were almost always confined to the worlds of sports and music. Year after year I would survey my students, and year after year the overwhelming majority of them aspired to become superstar athletes or entertainers because these were the only successful types of people they saw in the media who "looked just like them." In their minds, sports and entertainment were the only ways out of lives of grinding poverty—but the likelihood that they had the talents and predispositions necessary to make it in those highly competitive fields was always going to be slim. If they didn't become professional athletes or entertainers, what kind of alternatives did they have? And how could I inspire them to work toward classroom excellence regardless?

The challenges I faced trying to inspire my students to dream big despite their circumstances was my motivation for writing *The Teacher 50: Critical Questions for Inspiring Classroom Excellence.* I want you to reflect upon your teaching practices and the overall learning environment you have created: How have these elements succeeded or failed to inspire your students?

The Teacher 50 complements my previous book, *The Principal 50.* It is intentionally short out of respect for classroom teachers' extremely busy schedules. The 50 reflective questions in this book are offshoots of one essential, overarching query: *How can I inspire excellence in my classroom?* This is the fundamental question that I want you to keep in the back of your mind at all times. After you've read *The Teacher 50* for the first time, I encourage you to regularly ask yourself the 50 questions as they relate to your daily practice. Remember: The more inspired your classroom, the greater the chances that your students will achieve excellence.

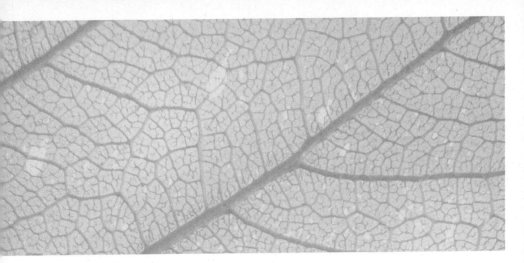

CHAPTER 1

Teacher Attitude

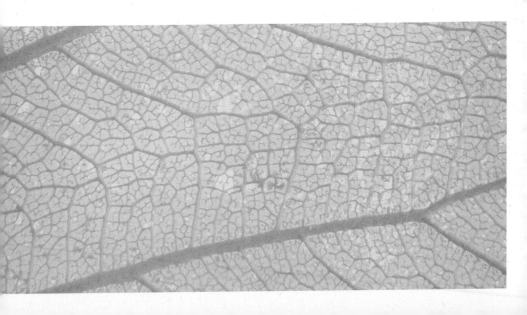

Q: Are My Students at an Advantage *Because* I Am Their Teacher?

An ongoing debate in the world of education revolves around the question of who or what has the biggest influence on a child's potential for classroom success. Some argue that students' home environments make the biggest difference; others argue for students' socioeconomic status, the overall school environment, or the classroom teacher. I contend that all these variables have a significant influence on students—but none more so than students' teachers.

The amount of influence that classroom teachers have on student success can't be overstated. They are the ultimate difference-makers—the game-changers who can either make or break their students. It's pivotal to understand this influence. When you walk into your classroom every day, confident that you are the number-one determinant of the success or failure of your students, you are ready to ensure that optimal student learning will occur. When you take it a step further and internalize the idea that your students *will* be successful *because* you are their teacher, your students are in the best possible position to achieve success. I'm not promoting egotism here—I'm promoting the willful, inspiring attitude necessary for your students to experience classroom excellence.

Q: Why Do I Teach, Anyway?

One day, it occurred to me that every single word in the dictionary has a meaning—or, you might say, a *purpose.* And as with words in the dictionary, all teachers should also be able to define the purpose of their work. Teachers who come to class every day with no purpose are like words in the dictionary with a blank space where the definitions should be.

What is your definition of your work's meaning and purpose? Go beyond generalizations like making a difference in the lives of children or preparing them for the future. What is your *specific* purpose for teaching your students? What drives you to get up in the morning and report to your classroom every day? What drives you to continue to do the work that you do despite the challenges that you face every day?

When I worked as a classroom teacher I was driven by many different factors, but at my core, my ultimate *purpose* was *to motivate, educate, and empower children*—with an emphasis on *empower*. To empower children is to make them stronger, more confident, and better able to control their lives (and to turn the corner if they're on the wrong track). Far too many students, particularly those from disadvantaged backgrounds, don't feel empowered to take charge of the direction of their lives.

Now think about *your* specific purpose for the work that you do—your personal definition of teaching. Let this purpose drive everything that you say and do from now on as you work to inspire classroom excellence.

Q: How Badly Do I Want to See My Students Succeed?

When I conduct professional development workshops with educators, I typically begin by asking attendees, "What are the challenges, obstacles, pressures, demands, and adversities that you face in your classrooms daily? Put another way: What keeps you up at night?" The teachers' responses can sometimes be overwhelmingly emotional. I recall several times having to hold back tears as I listened to teachers with tears in their own eyes. At one workshop not too long ago, a teacher confided to me that what kept her up at night was knowing that one of her students lived in a rat-infested apartment. She told me that this knowledge made her particularly determined to ensure that her student would become a success. These moments speak volumes to me: They are glimpses into the hearts of teachers who take the pressures and demands of their jobs home and to bed every evening.

My point in asking teachers to share during workshops is to gauge how badly they want to see their students succeed in the face of sometimes overwhelming odds. How badly do *you* want to see *your* students succeed? How badly do you want to be prepared to surmount all the obstacles that you'll face, day in and day out, in your classroom? Are you up to the challenge of meeting the needs of a diverse group of learners? Do you have the will to be a great teacher for all your students? Are you willing to learn all you have to know to connect with every student in your classroom? What adjustments can you make on a daily basis to meet all your students' academic, social, and emotional needs? How do you ensure that your students remain fired up for success in life?

You have got to want your kids to succeed at a gut level. You have got to be practically obsessed with helping them discover and exploit their potential for greatness, and you have got to be passionate about their success.

Q: Where Will My Students Be 10 Years from Now as a Result of Having Me as Their Teacher?

I once had a very interesting conversation with a 4th grade teacher about her daily classroom challenges. "Principal Kafele, I am working entirely too hard," she said. "My principal gives me all the students that no one else wants and then expects me to perform miracles with them."

I told this teacher that her principal must have a great deal of confidence in her abilities and asked her what kind of results she was getting with her students.

"I have the highest test scores in the building," she said, "but I work harder than most of my colleagues to get them because I teach the most challenging students."

I was intrigued by the teacher's response. Although she had the most challenging students in the building, they consistently outscored everyone else. I asked her how this could be.

"There are a lot of reasons," she said, "but I will narrow it down to one word: *vision*. I can 'see' their success before they walk into my classroom—before we even embark on the first lesson. I see them doing great things with their lives years after they leave my classroom."

She hit the nail on the head. This teacher didn't see her students solely as 4th graders, but also as the adults that they would eventually become. She had a vision of where they would one day be as a result of the work she was putting in daily. Her vision of what her students could become tomorrow inspired how she treated them today.

What is your vision for your students? What will your students become as adults? Where will they be 10 years from now as a result of the year they spend with you? You must see beyond your students' current circumstances and into their futures. Teaching without a sense of vision shortchanges children, forcing us to teach solely on mitigating the concerns of the present.

Q: Do My Students See Me as an Example of Who and What They Can Become?

Over the years, the term "rock star" has been used to denote people who are particularly good at their jobs. Are you a "rock star" in your classroom? Do you perform at such high levels that your students recognize your greatness and see you as an example to emulate? Are you a role model for your students? You will serve your students best if you're a dynamite teacher who regularly performs miracles in the classroom, such as teaching students who may have been written off by colleagues and helping them to become high academic performers.

Many educators either forget or are unaware that they are role models. Remember, students are watching you model appropriate behavior even when it appears that they aren't. And although it may not be apparent unless you pay close attention, many students probably see their relationships with you as among the most significant in their lives. How do you think your students see you? What is their perception of you as a teacher and as a person? Are you aware of your status as a role model? Do they see examples in you of who and what they can become? If not, why not? I strongly encourage you to always be conscious of what you say and do in the presence of students because they are "recording" it all. Your actions and words—even ones you might not otherwise give a second thought to—play an absolutely crucial role in shaping students.

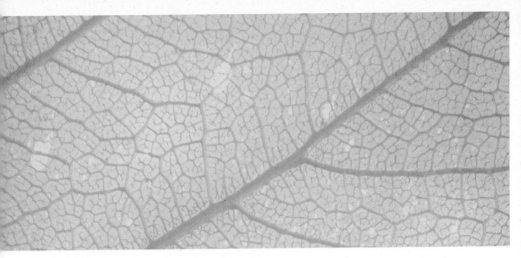

CHAPTER 2

Student Motivation

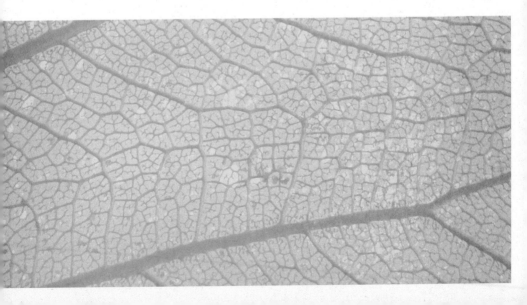

Q: What Is My Signature Classroom Move?

Think of the word *signature*. What comes to your mind? The written signature we use to endorse checks and seal contracts is unique to each of us; it is ours and ours alone. But we can also use the word to describe individual specialties for which we are known—a signature recipe, for example. Being an avid basketball fan, I think of the signature moves that various players are known for on the court.

In the classroom, my signature move was always delivering an opening message to my students every morning. Because I knew that many of them went home every afternoon to difficult environments that sapped them of their sense of hope, I felt it was my purpose to inspire and empower them, and I also knew that subject knowledge alone would never do the trick. So, every morning, I would deliver an inspiring and empowering address that set the tone for the rest of the day.

What is *your* signature move in the classroom? What is that thing—that one activity, strategy, word, expression—that sets you apart from the rest—that secret weapon that keeps all your students inspired in the face of adversity?

Q: Do I "Bring the Fire" into My Classroom Every Day?

Fire—the energy, excitement, and enthusiasm that you bring to the classroom every day—is a vital component of your teaching repertoire. Because it's your professional responsibility to ensure that your students remain engaged and inspired to work on even the driest subject material, you must be prepared to spark life into your lessons every single day.

Fire should not be confused with charisma, which not everyone possesses in large amounts. Fire is about energy and relish for the work of teaching. It is paramount that your students see evidence of your fire every time they're in class with you. They must see in your practice that you are truly passionate both about the work that you do and about them as your students.

I like telling teachers that they need to get in there and destroy the competition: *negative attitudes*. Fire can help you to eliminate negative student attitudes toward school and life. Children simply can't soar when they don't feel positive and uplifted. Do you bring the fire to your classroom every day? Can your students sense the fire burning within you? Is the fire—the enthusiasm for the work of learning—spreading to them?

Q: Do I Believe That My Students Can Fly?

For a while in the late 1990s, R. Kelly's hit song "I Believe I Can Fly" was played at every one of the many graduations I attended as a speaker. I cannot tell you how many children I have heard sing this song over the years. As I would sit on those stages listening to the children sing, I often wondered to myself if they truly believed what the lyrics were saying, and if their teachers and parents believed it as well. Students *must* believe they can fly if they are going to maximize their potential.

We have all been confronted with unmotivated students who don't seem to understand the importance of hard work and who view their entire school experience as largely irrelevant to their lives. How do we respond to these students? Are they to blame for their indifference toward learning? Too often, teachers will pass immediate judgment on students due to such external factors as difficult home lives or low socioeconomic status. Assuming that such factors are impossible to surmount, these teachers will often neglect to even try to challenge and inspire students whom they deem to be lost causes. Tragically, the result is that otherwise brilliant students will go through school without being pushed toward excellence and permitted to exercise their option to fail. Teachers who base their practice on automatic negative assumptions clearly do not believe that their students can fly and are positioning their students not to believe it.

Forget about the external influences and concentrate on the students in the classroom, where they are all capable of lift off. Because *you* are their teacher, your students are going to soar—and failure is *not* an option! You need to believe emphatically that all your students can fly regardless of the circumstances outside the classroom door. Holding high expectations for your students is a way of showing your faith in them. You must expect excellence. You must expect greatness. You must expect extraordinary results.

Q: Have I Helped My Students to Put a Definition Next to Their Names?

Earlier in this book, I asked you to consider your purpose for teaching. Now I want to focus on your students. What are their purposes for learning? Does your own personal purpose for teaching have any effect on your students' purposes for learning? Are your students driven by their purposes? Do you lead your students in discussions about their purposes? How you answer these questions will go a long way toward determining how energized about learning your students will be.

Like teachers, students need to be able to define what they are in the classroom to do. And as a teacher, you must make it a priority to ensure that your students understand the importance of finding meaning in their academic lives. We are all fully aware of how easy it is for students to become distracted or tempted to engage in counterproductive behavior. Distraction comes easily to those who aren't driven by a purpose, which narrows students' focus and gets them thinking about what matters most. To develop this indispensable attribute, regularly engage your students in conversations about defining their purpose in the classroom.

Q: How Do I Prevent My Students from Wearing Blindfolds in My Classroom?

Are your goals for your students specific, measurable, attainable, realistic, and timely? Are they clearly posted in the classroom? Do you review them with your students on a regular basis? Are the goals accompanied by a written plan of action? If so, do you walk your plan every day? If you want your students to work toward excellence at all times, you must be able to answer an emphatic "Yes!" to these questions. Your students need to know that walking through life without goals is like intentionally putting on and walking around with a blindfold every day; they have no clear idea of where they're going.

In my workshops, I like to ask teachers how many of them require that their students predetermine their final grades for each subject. Most teachers don't do this, and I believe that's a mistake. How can we expect our students to achieve goals that were never set in the first place? Without goals in place, your students are going through school wearing blindfolds.

Goal setting is a bit like the Global Positioning System (GPS): the goal is the destination, the route is the plan, and the time of arrival is the deadline for achieving the goal. Make sure that your students have their own goal-setting procedures in place and that their goals are attached to desired grade outcomes. At the start of every marking period, have your students write their goals and plans and post them on a board labeled "Student Goals."

CHAPTER 3

Classroom Climate
and Culture

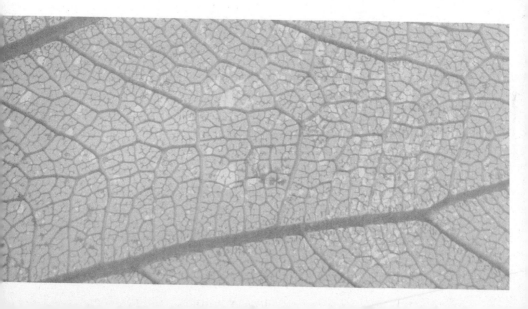

Q: Is My Classroom a "Bam!" Classroom?

A "Bam!" classroom is one that provides students with an over-whelmingly magical and memorable experience. In my capacity as a consultant, I eagerly seek out the "Bam!" classrooms in every building I visit. They're not hard to notice—they're the ones that give you that "Bam!" feeling as soon as you walk in the door. Is yours a "Bam!" classroom? Is the learning environment you provide for your students magical and memorable? "Bam!" classrooms nurture excellence so that learning can occur at the highest levels. They make students feel good about themselves and comfortable within the overall environment.

When I worked as a principal, I spent the bulk of my days going in and out of classrooms, and I was always especially conscious of the feeling I got when I walked in each door. I wanted to ensure that every classroom provided students with a sense of positivity and well-being—and each one did—but some felt truly magical. In these classrooms, students were valued and free to be themselves without having to conform to peer pressure; relationships abounded, and I could actually sense the caring and compassion in the air; and standards and expectations were set sky-high. In short, these were "Bam!" classrooms.

Q: What Is My Classroom's Way of Life?

Schools are microcosms of the outside world, with each classroom affording a glimpse at a unique culture. As in the world at large, classrooms are densely populated environments where people have to learn how to live together—how to communicate, relate, and resolve conflicts. All the people in a school are bound together by a particular vision and an overall structure of community.

When I worked as a classroom teacher, the culture of my classroom was a key and nonnegotiable element. I knew what I needed it to be at all times and it could not be dictated by the students—at least not until they internalized the culture that I had predetermined. You too must consider the culture of your classroom from the outset. You must walk in there on Day 1 already knowing what it will evolve into. You, the teacher, must be in control of the learning environment rather than letting it control you.

Your classroom's culture represents the way you and your students are living when you're together. It is your classroom's *way of life*. What is the culture—the way of life—of your classroom? Have your students contributed to it? Did the culture evolve organically, or did you have a preexisting idea that you worked toward realizing?

Q: What Is It About My Classroom That My Students Can't Wait to Come Back in the Morning?

I consider *intentionality* to be the most potent word in my professional lexicon. It is what gets us from striving for something to actually manifesting it. Virtually everything you do related to the social, emotional, and academic growth of your students is something that you must do on purpose; this intentionality must be more than evident to your students. You cannot wait for your classroom climate and culture to develop on their own—you must shape and mold them *intentionally.*

Imagine transcending traditional models to create an experience that is so stimulating and engaging for students that they are eager to return to your classroom day after day. When you believe that you can achieve these results and focus on doing so, you will be working with intentionality to inspire student excellence.

Are you intentional about the climate and culture—the mood and the way of life—of your classroom? Do you regularly and intentionally celebrate your students' achievements? Do you build strong intentional relationships with students and exhibit as much compassion as you can at all times? All these factors are essential to consider if you want to create a climate and a culture that enable your students to soar.

Q: Do I Teach *Math* or Do I Teach *Mathew?*

What is the real priority in your classroom: the subject matter or your students? Far too often, teachers get so caught up in the normal pressures of teaching to the test and covering the whole curriculum on time that they forget what truly matters: the children. You can never lose sight of your students being your priority. Ensuring your students' social, emotional, and academic growth is the reason you report to school every day; everything else is secondary.

So, do you teach *math,* or do you teach *Mathew?* You teach *math* to *Mathew,* of course, but is Mathew's well-being your foremost priority?

Q: Is My Classroom's Brand Identity Conducive to Learning at the Highest Levels?

Just as marketers and advertisers work hard to create a *brand identity* to sell their products, you too must work to develop and maintain a brand identity for your classroom. What distinguishes your learning space from all the others in your school? To what extent did you create your classroom's brand identity, and to what extent are you in control of it?

At a minimum, your classroom's brand identity is composed of

- Your *core beliefs* about both the practice of teaching and the process of learning;
- Your *core values* and *guiding principles* about what matters most for your students; and
- Your classroom's *purpose, mission,* and *vision.*

Your classroom's brand identity dictates your students' academic outcomes, their classroom behaviors, and their perceptions of the learning environment. At the same time, what's actually happening in the classroom is what ends up *defining* the brand identity—not simply what the teacher *says* or *hopes* is happening. It is incumbent upon you to ensure that you have in place a classroom brand identity that embraces nothing less than excellence for your students.

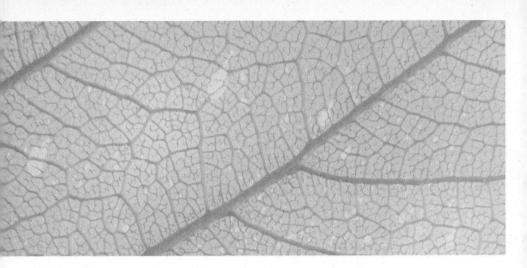

CHAPTER 4

Building
Relationships

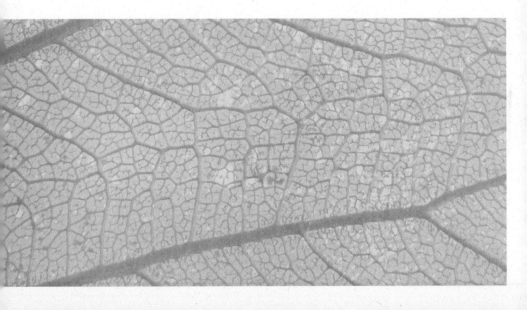

Q: Do I Know My Students Beyond the Dismissal Bell?

When I worked as a classroom teacher, I made familiarizing myself with my students' homes and neighborhoods a non-negotiable aspect of my practice. There was no way I could truly get to know my students well if I didn't understand the nature of their living environments. To this end, I visited as many of my students' homes as I possibly could. These visits allowed me to get to know my students and their parents quite well. When I became a principal, I continued my regular neighborhood and home visits—as the leader of the school, I wanted to know my students as deeply as I could. Even now, as an education consultant, I continue the practice: visiting the neighborhoods of the students at the schools with which I'm working. Prior to school visits, I make it a point to drive through the streets surrounding the school to get a general idea of the environment.

The schools that I work with are often in low-income urban or rural environments, and the students who go there are affected to varying degrees by the conditions of their surroundings. The circumstances of students' lives cannot prevent them from soaring to the highest heights, but they might necessitate students to work harder than peers in more privileged communities. Never lose sight of the fact that your students are shaped by where they're from.

How have you adapted to your students and to their environments? How have they adapted to your classroom? Are you acquainted with your students' homes and communities? The six to eight hours your students spend with you every weekday represent only a fraction of who they are. If you really want to know your students deeply so you can inspire them to achieve beyond their wildest dreams, be sure to get out and familiarize yourself with where they live.

Q: Am I Intimidated by Any of My Students, Their Parents, or the Community in Which They Reside?

It is a no-brainer that you as a classroom teacher should never exhibit any fear toward your students, regardless of their age or size. You must be able to remain in charge throughout all adverse situations. Students must perceive you as being in control at all times. If they can detect that you're fearful, it will be very difficult to maintain influence in your classroom.

The same argument applies to your attitude toward students' parents. Trust me, I am well aware that there are parents out there who can be disrespectful, overbearing, and downright hostile toward teachers. Despite parents' often blatant hostility, you must continue to demonstrate your authority and *not* lose your composure. If parents detect that you are intimidated by them, they will use this against you by continuing to be confrontational instead of working with you to find a middle ground so that you can work collaboratively for the benefit of the student.

As to the students' communities, I have had countless conversations with teachers over the years about their concerns for their students' safety in the urban neighborhoods where they live. As we delve deeper into the topic, it often becomes apparent that the teachers are concerned about their own safety as well. They might feel safe in the school environment, but not in the surrounding community. If you are in this kind of situation, I want to challenge you to fight any fear you may have and instead strive to understand the factors that have led to the current conditions. Reflect on the way poverty and the "isms" of the world have created the environment into which many of your students were born. Your students cannot afford for you to be intimidated by their neighborhoods because they are the products of their neighborhoods—in so many cases, it is all they know. When you fear their neighborhoods, you are essentially fearing *them*. When you criticize or condemn their neighborhoods, you are essentially criticizing and condemning them as well. Although these neighborhoods may be replete with challenges, the overwhelming majority of their residents are great people struggling to succeed against overwhelming odds. As a teacher, you can never lose sight of this reality.

Q: How Do My Students Perceive Me and My Treatment of Them?

Many years ago, when I was a principal, I had a student who made it very evident that she didn't particularly care for me. She didn't like what I stood for in my role of principal, and her feelings were so strong that she even had difficulty saying hello to me in the morning. I was very concerned about her perception, so I had to take time to reflect on the way I was portraying myself to her and her peers. I soon discovered that the problem wasn't me personally, but rather my title. The student in question had bad experiences with the leadership in her previous school and consequently put me in the same category. She felt that she wasn't respected as a student by her previous principal, and that I therefore didn't respect her either. This mattered a lot to me, and I set myself the goal of changing her perception of principals in general, which I hoped would lead her to change her perception of me specifically.

What are your students' perceptions of you? What are their perceptions of how you treat them? Both of these perceptions matter. It is very difficult to make solid connections with children when they perceive that we do not care about them. Our students need to know that we care about them first and foremost. What we say to them is simply not enough; our actions speak much louder than our words. For students to be in the position to maximize their potential, they need to be in classroom learning environments where teachers show that they care for them, like them, appreciate them, respect them, understand them, demonstrate empathy toward them, are patient with them, treat them equally and fairly, and display a solid commitment to their overall growth and development.

In my professional development workshops, I often ask teachers how they can gauge whether their students know that they care about them. As I always say, we can state at the workshop that we love our students, but if our students don't see that love in action—in the way that we communicate and interact with our students every single day—then it doesn't make a difference.

Q: To What Extent Am I Involved in My Students' Lives?

I often say that you can't teach your students if you don't know them. There is so much more to your students than who they are when they're sitting at their desks. In my hometown of

Jersey City, New Jersey, I know a teacher who takes his students far beyond the classroom to help them draw meaningful connections. He enrolls them in a plethora of different programs and engages them in a variety of activities in an effort to expand their horizons. In making these efforts, this teacher is able to have maximum involvement in his students' lives. The results are that he knows his students much better than he would if his relationships with them were restricted to the classroom, and this stronger bond leads to a higher probability that his students will listen to and learn from his lessons.

How well do you know your students? How well do your students know you? To what extent do you know your students beyond the dismissal bell? To what extent are you involved in your students' lives? One of the best ways to know your students is by intentionally forging relationships with them, which means having some level of involvement in their lives beyond the content areas that you teach. Many students, particularly at the middle and high school levels, are involved in extracurricular activities. To what extent are you a part of these activities? If your students are involved in sports, to what extent do you attend their games? If they are involved in theater, how often do you go to their plays? Making yourself visible to your students outside classroom hours is a vital way to establish deep relationships with your students.

Q: How Often Do My Students and I "Break Bread" Together?

One very common concern that teachers often raise to me is that they simply don't have enough time in the day to get to know their students as well as they'd like. They talk about the pressures and demands of their work and how they spend so much of their day on responsibilities beyond the scope of teaching.

When I was a 5th grade teacher, I faced my own set of pressures and demands way beyond the scope of classroom instruction. I, too, wanted to get to know my students better than I could during instructional time. To that end, I would spend considerable after-school time in their homes and neighborhoods—but the biggest breakthrough was my lunch period. I decided to spend all my lunch periods with my students in an attempt to create as familial an atmosphere as I could. Every day, I ate lunch with students either in the cafeteria or in my classroom—sometimes with everyone, other times in small groups. Although I encouraged them to talk to one another about whatever they wanted, I also led conversations on certain days, trying to learn as much as I could about what they were interested in outside school. Using my lunch period in this way allowed me to get to know my students very well. Having lunch with my students became a part of the culture of my classroom and didn't impose on my students' free time or privacy. When I became an administrator, I continued to meet with my students during lunch, identifying different tables to sit at in the cafeteria and discuss any subject imaginable with students.

Do you "break bread" with your students by sitting with them at lunch? If so, how often? If not, why not? Of course, we all need our own pockets of free time, but do bear in mind that your students' lunch period is an invaluable time for you to get to know them, bond with them, and establish a rapport with them beyond teaching and learning. The conversations should be light and easygoing enough that they don't feel like work.

Always keep in mind that cultivating solid relationships with students is key to helping them maximize learning. However much time you have at your disposal toward building better relationships with your students, be sure to take full advantage of it.

CHAPTER 5

Classroom
Instruction

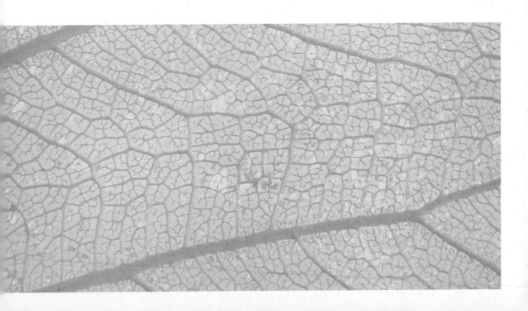

Q: How Do I Know Which Instructional Strategies Work Best with Each of My Students?

I often reflect upon my years as a grade school student. Starting in late elementary school, my academic performance spiraled from average to horrible by the time I got to high school. I didn't bounce back until I got to college and became self-motivated. Many of my peers had similar trajectories. Today, I am able to look back on my K–12 experience through the lens of a practitioner. There is no doubt in my mind that the instructional strategies my grade-school teachers employed were not conducive to bringing out the best in me or my peers. We were subjected to dreadfully boring lectures and forced to sit in rigidly demarcated rows, with many of us placed in the rear of the classroom. If only my teachers had known more about how students actually learn and process information.

As a consultant, I continue to see the same counterproductive instructional strategies that my peers and I endured decades ago in countless classrooms across the country. In these environments, I often see students who are disengaged, bored, and disruptive. There is little in place to hold their attention and to keep them engaged in the learning process.

To ascertain which instructional strategies work best with each of your students, you must first and foremost know your students, as discussed in Chapter 4. You can't connect with them if you don't know them. You have got to build relationships with them. In doing so, you are putting yourself in a better position to get to know how they learn. You can't assume that they're going to be engaged by a lecture format if they aren't auditory learners, for example.

How do you ensure that your students are all engaged in the learning process? How do you ensure that you are implementing the most appropriate instructional strategies in your classroom? As the classroom teacher, you must make it a priority to discover how your students learn so you can set them up for classroom excellence.

Q: Who Are the True Stars of the Show in My Classroom?

It is not uncommon to go into a classroom anywhere in the country and find quiet, disciplined students sitting in rows listening intently to a teacher's lecture. In these classrooms, teachers are the "stars of the show." Although their students will almost certainly learn something, I question whether they will attain maximum results. Classrooms are composed of students with so many different learning styles and ability levels that I cannot imagine this approach connecting with all learners. Auditory learners will probably do just fine, but what about everyone else? Why are the other students unintentionally excluded from the learning process? Typically, when students have trouble understanding the material or appear to be disengaged, we ask them questions: We question their focus, we question their work ethic, we question their seriousness, we question their cognitive ability, and we question their potential for success. All too often, these students wind up in less challenging learning environments or even in special-needs classrooms. Why? Because in their classrooms, they're not the stars of the show: They're not receiving the attention that they require for success, and their needs—academic, social, and emotional—are not being met. In these classrooms, it is the teachers who receive the attention.

From pre-K through high school, you must always remember that your students are the stars of the classroom—not spectators, extras, or even co-stars, but the central protagonists in a student-centered learning environment. The classroom is all about them.

Are your students the stars of your classroom? Is your classroom environment student centered? Do your students receive opportunities to learn that are based on their unique strengths and learning styles? Do your instructional strategies enable your students to be fully engaged in their own learning? Do they enable your students to experience academic rigor in a learning environment that is fun, stimulating, and engaging? Do you take into consideration all the learners in your classroom? You must ensure that the instructional strategies you implement enable your students to be the stars of the show in the classroom.

Q: How Do I Connect Learning Across the Content Areas?

I have the privilege of regularly interacting with many different teachers who experience very different types of challenges. Many of them—typically urban and rural teachers working in underprivileged communities—face challenges so extreme that they end up leaving the teaching profession. At the opposite end of the spectrum, I meet a lot of teachers who know nothing about the challenges that urban and rural teachers face. But one challenge that all these teachers face—regardless of where they teach—is a lack of cohesion among the content areas, particular at the middle and high school levels. Ideally, students would clearly be able to see how language arts, mathematics, science, and social studies all connect with one another rather than learning about them as totally separate, compartmentalized fields of study.

How do you connect the content areas so that your students can see the correlations? Do you take an interdisciplinary approach to instruction? Do you ensure that learning is holistic for your students? It is important for your students to understand how entwined the content areas really are.

Q: Do I Take into Account That No Two of My Students Are Alike?

One of the biggest concerns that teachers express to me is class size, especially in urban schools. Large class sizes create an assortment of challenges for teachers, particularly when it comes to differentiating instruction for students. Although differentiating instruction can be a challenge even in small classrooms, when the head count begins to approach 30 it can become a nightmare. Still, if students are going to succeed academically, teachers must engage in differentiation.

I often remind teachers that no two students are alike despite any outward similarities and that we put them at a disadvantage when we act as though they are alike. A typical classroom is filled with many different learning styles, ability levels, interest levels, needs, and aspirations; you must take all those differences into account when you prepare your lessons. Too many students either fail or underachieve *not* because they lack ability, but because their teachers have failed to identify how they learn best. As the classroom teacher, it is absolutely imperative that you discover how your students learn best and teach them accordingly.

I get the challenges of differentiation. I get that it is far easier to use whole-group instruction in a large classroom and that it has its place—but it should never be the end-all. At best, it is a bridge to more personalized instruction later on.

Do you consider the unique learning styles, ability levels, interest levels, needs, and aspirations of each of your students? Do you understand that no two of your students are alike? Understanding your students' individual differences and teaching them in a way that takes these into account is of the utmost importance if you want students to thrive academically.

Q: Does My Teaching Address the 21st Century Student?

I often think about the students I taught from 1988 to 1997 and compare them with the students I led as a principal from 1998 to 2011—two different sets of students with vastly different technological experiences. The first group's vocabulary did not include the words *cell phone, e-mail, Internet, social media,* or *app.* In fact, these students were lucky if they had one PC per classroom or access to a computer lab. By contrast, the students in the second group faced an onslaught of new technology over a very short span of time. As a result, students in this group were in many ways far ahead not only of the students in the first group, but of their teachers as well. Through the use of new technology, these students were exposed to a world that the previous cohort knew nothing about.

The Internet has brought the entire world to your students' fingertips—both the good and the bad. They are aware of and have instant access to endless categories of data that students 20 years ago simply couldn't access. Love or hate the Internet, it is influencing everything your students say and do.

How are you adapting to your students' use of new technology? How are you keeping up with these students? How are you holding their interest? How are you keeping them from getting bored in class and with school? Because these students are conditioned to having instant access to information, they often desire immediate gratification. Some have argued that students today have a much shorter attention span than previous generations as a result of the technological advances. The world we knew 20 years ago is not the world that your students are experiencing today. The pace is much faster, and as educators, we must keep up with it.

Does your teaching reflect the realities of students today? Is technology an integral part of your practice in your classroom? Are you technologically literate? Are you using technology in a way that connects to your students' backgrounds and skill levels? If you want to inspire excellence in your classroom, be sure that your teaching practices reflect the experiences of the students you teach.

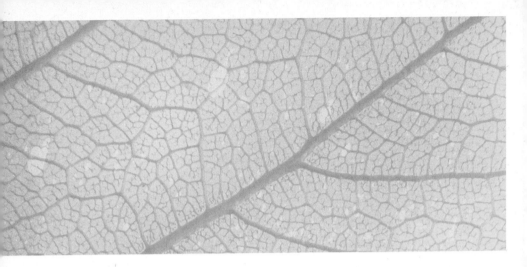

CHAPTER 6

Cultural
Responsiveness

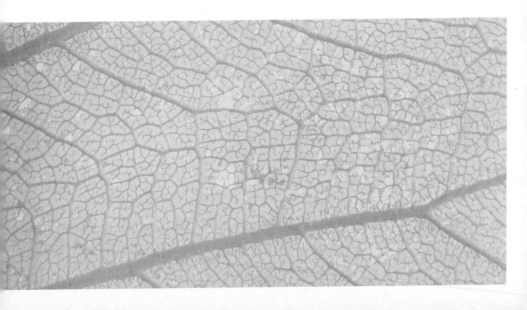

Q: Do I Consider My Students' Cultural Backgrounds When I Plan Instruction?

This question of the cultural backgrounds of students is very dear to my heart. I truly believe that it is at the core of everything I have done and will continue to do in education. All teachers should be willing to consider their students' identities beyond their names on the class roster.

I liken culturally responsive teaching and learning to a class picture. If you were to distribute a copy of your class picture to every student in your classroom, chances are that each one would look for himself or herself first and then look for friends. Now, let's suppose that the picture has several students cut out of it. When your students receive their copies, the students who are missing from the picture will probably be very disappointed. When curriculum and instruction fail to address the cultural and historical identities of all learners in the classroom, the students whose backgrounds have been ignored are as disappointed as they'd be if they'd been cut out of a class picture. They wonder, "Where am *I* in this lesson? What does this lesson have to do with *me*?"

In what ways does your instruction consider the cultural backgrounds of your students? In what ways does your instruction enable them to see themselves in the lessons you teach? Do your students feel that their cultures are being addressed in your lessons? In what ways is learning relevant to the cultural identities of your students? I urge you to consider each of these questions and the ones that follow as you prepare to teach your lessons.

Q: How Do I Infuse My Lessons with the History and Culture of My Students?

I have been an educator for 28 years. In that time, my thinking has evolved on many issues, but on one I have remained firm and unwavering: the importance of infusing students' historical and cultural backgrounds into classroom lessons.

Culturally responsive teaching is necessary because the majority culture in any society is usually explored fully in classrooms while underrepresented cultures are not. The most prominent examples of underrepresented cultures in the United States, and the ones I've had the most experience with in my years as an educator, are those of black and Latino students. The histories of these two communities have been distorted, neglected, marginalized, or omitted from the history books for generations; their true stories have not been told and subsequently remain a mystery to children all over the country.

Among the most fundamental questions that we can ask a youngster are, "Who are you?" "What is the historical context of your cultural identity?" "What stories in history is your cultural identity associated with?" and "What have your people contributed to the world?" Though Latinos and people of African descent have extensive histories and have made enormous contributions to the world, many of the children in these communities aren't aware of the particulars because the information hasn't been taught in the classroom. And not only are *they* unaware, their peers from other cultural backgrounds are also unaware.

What, then, is your role as the teacher relative to cultural responsiveness? First and foremost, you have to know about your students' historical identities. I understand that this is a tall order, but I also believe that it's necessary. When your students don't know who they are historically, they essentially don't know a large part of themselves and lack a solid foundation upon which to stand and grow as learners. Knowing the historical realities behind your students' cultural backgrounds will allow you to teach your students where they come from and be confident in their identities as they learn—a key factor in inspiring classroom excellence for all. It's worth noting that teaching your students' histories should not be limited to history class, but should be touched upon in classes across the subject areas.

Q: Do I Ensure That My Students Identify Culturally with the Lessons I Teach?

As I mentioned previously, it is difficult for students to learn when they don't see the relevance of the content to their own lives. Your students must be able to relate culturally with the lessons that you teach. In practice, this means that lesson planning cannot be confined to developing great lessons for hypothetical generic students—rather, it must be informed by your students' specific cultural backgrounds.

The likelihood is that your classroom includes diverse learners from multiple cultural backgrounds and experiences. A one-size-fits-all lesson is simply not going to connect with them all. To meet the learning needs of your diverse learners, you have got to know and understand them, which includes knowing and understanding them culturally. And as you get to know and understand them, you are putting yourself in much better position to connect with them culturally and thereby inspire classroom excellence.

Q: How Do I Demonstrate My Sensitivity to the Racial and Ethnic Diversity of My Students?

Over the years, I have had some very intense conversations with educators over whether they "see" the race and ethnicity of their students. Although I applaud those who say that they are colorblind when it comes to their students, I also remind them that society is not. In fact, society will see a student's race or ethnicity before anything else. We live in a world replete with judgments, generalizations, stereotypes, and "isms." Your students must be prepared not only to exist within the confines of this world, but also to soar within it.

How will you prepare your diverse student population to meet the challenges that they're bound to face in the real world? How will you prepare them to overcome the obstacles that race and ethnicity might present for them? How will you even broach the sensitive topic of potential prejudice? Your students will need you to demonstrate a sensitivity to the challenges that they may face due to their backgrounds or skin color, and the best way to begin is to acknowledge that the challenges exist rather than to ignore them. Forge relationships and create open lines of communication with your students that enable you to prepare them for success in the real world after they graduate. Demonstrating proficiency in the subject areas and on state standardized assessments is not enough—your students must also be prepared to effectively surmount obstacles they might encounter due to their race or ethnicity.

Q: Am I Willing to Learn All That I Can About My Students' Cultures?

When I began as a teacher, I said little if anything to my colleagues when I ventured into the teacher's lounge unless they spoke to me first—but my ears were wide open. What I learned in that room was an eye opener: The student body was 95 percent black and 5 percent Latino, and fully 90 percent of the kids received free or reduced lunch. The teaching staff was divided evenly between black and white teachers.

In the first few months of my first year, I would go into the teacher's lounge and just listen, seldom saying a word. I heard things about the children we were there to serve that have stayed with me to this day, from both the black and white teachers—namely, constant criticism and complaints about the students and their parents. A lot of what I heard was down-right ugly. I thought to myself, "How can these individuals call themselves teachers when they express sentiments like these? How will they ever be able to motivate their students if these are their true feelings?" What I heard made me very angry, and soon I decided to stay out of the teacher's lounge for the remainder of my career.

As I grew in the profession, I reflected on the things I'd heard teachers say in those first few months. Over time, as I came to understand the profound effect that culture has on our attitudes, behaviors, choices, and so on, I was able to conclude that my colleagues weren't bad people; they suffered from a lack of knowledge about the very students they were supposed to serve. Put simply, they didn't know them, they didn't understand them, and they didn't relate to them. They knew their students' names and a few details, but they couldn't understand or relate to their cultural backgrounds. They didn't understand how their students communicated, how they behaved, or how they joked around—that is, they didn't understand how their students thought, which of course profoundly affected how they learned. These teachers didn't understand life in the inner city and how it shapes students' dispositions—hence the criticisms and complaints.

As the classroom teacher, do you know your students? Do you know who they are culturally? Do you know how their own cultures affect who they are in your classroom? Having a different cultural background from you doesn't make students inferior, it just means that their life experiences are not the same as yours. It is your responsibility to make it a priority to really get to know your students beyond who they are when they are seated at their desks. You have to learn who they are culturally by forging solid relationships with them and demonstrating compassion toward them at all times. Understanding how your students' experiences have shaped their lives is absolutely essential for inspiring them to excel.

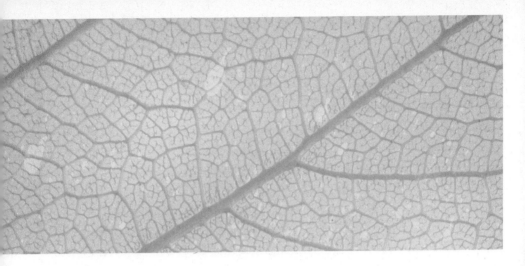

CHAPTER 7

Teacher
Accountability

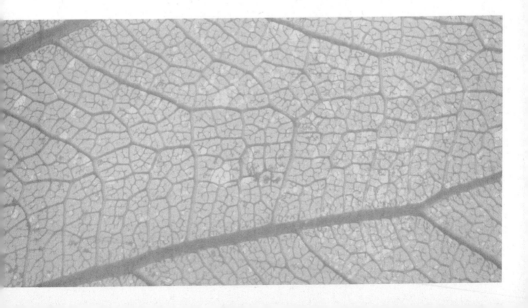

Q: Do My Students Have the Option of Failing in My Classroom?

One day during a trip to a school in the Midwest, I spent the morning visiting classrooms with the principal. Between each visit, we would discuss our observations in the hallway. As we walked around, I kept seeing the same motto on signs affixed to the school walls: "Failure is not an option!" Although I didn't mention the signs to the principal, I certainly made a note of them. Quite frankly, I had never seen so many signs with that one phrase on them in a single school; they were in every classroom and throughout the hallways. I was very impressed that failure as a non-option was a deliberate theme at this school.

When we were done with our observations and returned to the principal's office to debrief, I brought up the signs. I shared with the principal how I felt seeing them and how impressed I was that they were an integral part of the overall climate of the school.

"We're not about failure here," said the principal. "Failure is not an option in our school, starting with me—the principal."

Impressive indeed, but I thought I would take the liberty to challenge the principal and stretch his thinking a bit.

"I admire your drive to ensure that failure isn't a reality in your school," I said, "but the fact of the matter is that based on your current data, you have an abundance of students who are in fact failing and thereby exercising their *option* to fail. How do you explain this in the context of your motto?"

The principal appeared a bit perplexed by my question. After a moment of silence, he explained to me that *philosophically* the students do not have the option to fail, and that the school as a whole had deemed failure to be unacceptable, but that they had a long way to go to make the theme a reality.

Although I tend to agree that, in the long run, failure should not be an option for any student, some degree of short-term failure is actually welcome as it serves as a learning experience, allowing students to figure out what does and doesn't work moving forward. It's the long-term failure that we shouldn't tolerate: the giving up, the quitting, the clocking out.

Your role matters in ensuring that long-term failure is never an option. You must truly believe that your students will not fail in your classroom because you are the teacher and your success is tied to the success of your students. This is the game-changing mindset—a commitment to ensuring that the option to fail no longer exists in your classroom. You must hold yourself accountable for eliminating long-term failure by elevating your practice so that your vision of student excellence becomes a reality. Because your students' success flows directly from your success as a teacher, you must commit to avoid blaming the students, their parents, or socioeconomic factors for any failure that may occur. Put simply, your students' success or failure rests with *you*.

Q: Do I Hold Myself Accountable for Student Failure?

I have a fascination with reading proverbs from different countries and cultures around the world. I particularly enjoy reading them for the wisdom and life lessons they provide. One I stumbled upon many years ago is an African proverb that has actually guided my thinking and my practice as an educator for years: "He who cannot dance will say the drum is bad." When I read this proverb for the first time, it immediately resonated with me. Essentially, the proverb exhorts us to stop making excuses for our failures and shortcomings. If we were to update it for the present, the proverb might read: "He who can't dance will say the DJ isn't playing his song." Of course, the music isn't the issue—personal accountability is.

When your students fail to measure up to your expectations, do you say "the drum is bad"? There are many factors outside of your own teaching that you might blame for your students' failures. It's very easy to blame parents and the neighborhood environment, for example. But pointing the finger is not going to turn your students into success stories. Students in classrooms where teachers hold themselves completely accountable for their students' successes or failures are much likelier to perform better than those with teachers who would rather blame variables other than themselves.

How do you feel when your students fail? How do you hold yourself accountable? What adjustments do you make to your practice? Some failure is inevitable. The question is, what is your attitude when failure occurs, and how do you change your approach to decrease the probability of its recurrence?

Q: Am I Willing to Accept Responsibility and Accountability for My Students' Successes *and* Failures?

A willingness to accept responsibility and accountability for your students' successes is easy enough; it essentially speaks to your confidence as your students' teacher. As easy as it is to claim victories for yourself, it still takes audacity to attribute your students' achievements to your efforts—yet you absolutely must. It is absolutely imperative that you see within yourself the skill, ability, and talent to bring out the best in all your students.

Of course, willingness to accept responsibility and accountability for students' failures is much harder. When I was a classroom teacher, the odds against my students performing well were sky-high. I could easily have blamed poverty alone for my students' failures, as many of my students came from challenging socioeconomic environments. But I didn't let my students' conditions at home deter me one iota. Rather, I resolved that I would hold myself personally responsible for the successes and failures of all my students regardless of their lives outside the classroom.

The same must hold true for you. You have got to be willing to accept responsibility and accountability for your students' failures. Why? Because when you do, there is a much higher probability that you are going to do whatever it takes to grow professionally as you work to address your students' challenges. Your students may fail now and then, but your commitment to their success must be so strong that you will ensure that any one failure is not repeated.

Q: Do I Reject Poverty as a Legitimate Excuse for Failure?

Poverty is obviously a major obstacle for students to overcome if they want to succeed in the classroom. The effects of poverty are very real and often overwhelming; students who have to endure poverty shoulder a burden that those raised in more privileged conditions will never be able to fully comprehend or appreciate. In my interactions with teachers, I continue to be amazed that there are so many—both new and veteran, in urban and rural school districts—who are unaware of the difficulties that many of their students have to endure every day. At the same time, I interact with a lot of teachers who *do* understand because they see their students' difficulties first-hand; they venture out into their neighborhoods and homes to see clearly what their students go through.

What are your thoughts about poverty? Do you reject it as a legitimate excuse for failure? As the classroom teacher, do you have the skills necessary to help your students overcome the adverse effects of low socioeconomic status? Poverty is simply not a legitimate excuse for failure. Although I encourage you to recognize that it exists, you should never blame it for your students' poor performance.

I want you to be able to empathize as best you can with your economically disadvantaged students. You must always believe that no matter their circumstances, they are going to thrive in your classroom because you are their teacher. Your classroom should be an oasis for these students, a magical environment where they feel special and valued because of the way you treat them. You must create a learning environment where every single student feels inspired toward excellence by your actions and attitude. Though poverty is real, it cannot dictate student outcomes. You need to envision all your students succeeding, and you must always see yourself as the single most important determinant of their success.

Q: What Does My Mirror Say About My Effectiveness as a Teacher?

One of my favorite sports is football. I particularly enjoy the preparations for a game. I suppose the game itself should be the most important aspect, but because I tend to look at life through the lens of an educator, the preparations take on more relevance for me than the actual game itself. During the regular football season, all the games are played on Sunday except for one that is played on Monday night. For the teams that play on Sunday, Monday morning is an important time to prepare for the following week's game. This is when teams study, break down, analyze, and dissect video of the game they played the day before, zeroing in on every aspect of their performance. Reviewing game film gives players and coaches the opportunity to learn from the strengths, weaknesses, and mistakes of Sunday's game. Actual preparation for the next week's game will not occur until everyone has had an opportunity to watch the game film.

Just as the football players must study their game film, you, too, must study your own version of a game film for your week's lessons—only in your case, the "game film" is actually your reflection in the mirror. At the end of every day, you must make time to study your "film" before returning to the classroom. As you look at your reflection, you must "run the video" of your teaching from the start of the day to the end. Review every aspect of your day in the classroom, including your overall attitude. Just let the "video" run, then run it again, this time using a self-assessment process. Determine what worked, what didn't, and what you need to improve upon. Evaluate yourself honestly. No need to wait for an official assessor—your mirror can handle the job.

When you're finished with your self-assessment, you must self-adjust. Consider what changes you will make going into the next day's lessons. In football, there's no such thing as a perfect game—there will always be areas that necessitate improvement. If teams don't adjust their performance, they are fulfilling Einstein's definition of insanity—doing the same thing over and over and expecting different results. The same principles apply to your practice in the classroom. You have to reflect on and assess your performance daily so that you can make the necessary adjustments. Failure to do so will prevent you from moving forward in your practice as a better teacher.

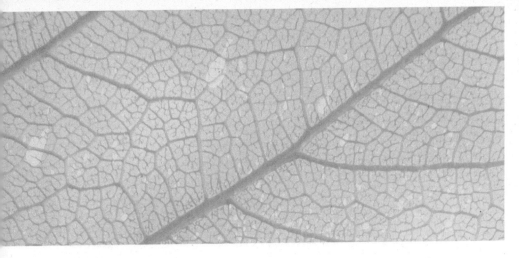

CHAPTER 8

Planning and Organization

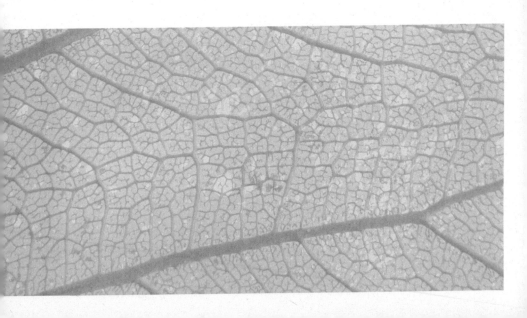

Q: To What Extent Do I Prepare Beyond My Lesson Plans?

All through my years as a classroom teacher, I took lesson planning very seriously. I actually looked forward to my Sunday mornings and afternoons, when I would sit at a table planning and envisioning my lessons for the coming week. I knew that the success or failure of my students hinged on my Sunday planning. My lesson plans enabled me to foresee the entire week and provided me with a blueprint to ensure optimal learning for my students.

Of course, planning lessons isn't optional—it's a requirement of the job. Typically, teachers submit lesson plans to an evaluator of record on a designated day. However, to be optimally effective in the classroom, I encourage teachers to make an additional set of plans that they don't share with the evaluator: individualized plans to address each student's specific needs. These plans don't need to be developed in conjunction with the lesson plans; indeed, they can be ongoing. What's important is preparing to meet the individual needs of each student in the classroom.

How important are your lesson plans to your daily practice? How much energy and effort do you put into developing them each week? To what extent do you prepare beyond the lesson plans that you share with your evaluator of record? Do you plan for each individual student? I firmly believe that your students will perform at much higher levels if you maintain individual plans for them that you update as needed. What does each student require of you? What are the learning needs of each student you teach, and how are they being met? Your students will benefit immensely from receiving this kind of individual attention from you.

Q: How Does Data Drive My Practice?

I am known to say that everything under the sun is data. The keys on my computer as I type this sentence are data, as are the fingers I'm using to type. The question is, how do we recognize data? How do we acknowledge it? How do we interpret it? How do we analyze it? How do we use it? How do we incorporate it? What does it tell us? What do we learn from it?

How does data drive your practice? Not just your instruction, but your practice as a whole. Data related to student attendance, class participation, homework completion, assessment results, and disciplinary actions are all important to consider. Do these types of data drive your decision making? Do they inform your practice? Do they dictate instructional strategies?

As the classroom teacher, you must use all the data at your disposal. The data tells the story of where you and your students stand at any given juncture. When you examine the information carefully, the decisions you make are grounded in the reality of your classroom; if you ignore the data, you're moving against reality. As you plan for each day, do not allow emotions, instincts, or assumptions to drive your practice. Be sure to use all the data streams at your disposal to ensure that all your students have an opportunity to succeed in the classroom.

Q: Have I Developed Expertise in My Content Area?

When I lead motivational assemblies for students, I regularly tell them that "average" is not good enough; they must strive to be the best versions of themselves that they can possibly be. Far too many young people settle for less and proceed through life tapping into only a mere fraction of their potential for greatness.

The same is true for teachers: we cannot afford to be average at what we do. Rather, we must be intentionally great at what we do, because our work is among the most important there is: we are preparing children for adulthood. Children deserve, require, and expect teachers to be experts both in the practice of teaching and in the actual content areas that they teach.

Are you an expert in your content area? How important is it to you that you be one? How much time do you devote to perfecting your practice? How much time do you devote to reflecting on, assessing, and adjusting your content-area expertise? Just as you must know your students as well as you possibly can, you must also know your content area inside and out. You must strive to be the go-to person for your subject at your school. Possessing a deep knowledge and understanding of your content area better positions your students for success in the classroom and beyond.

Q: What Role Does Child Development Theory Play in My Overall Planning?

Here's an area that really doesn't get the amount of attention it deserves. Child development theory is not an especially popular topic of discussion, but it should be. Ask yourself: Are the instructional materials that you use developmentally appropriate for your students? What about the strategies you employ? To what extent are you even aware of where your students are developmentally? Child development theory has to be the basis for your repertoire of classroom strategies if you want to put your students in the best possible position to excel at learning.

Q: Am I Highly Organized as a Teacher?

Given the overwhelming number of responsibilities that accompany the practice of teaching, organizational skills are absolutely indispensable. In my seminars, teachers often express concerns about the enormous amount of paperwork that accompanies their practice and how little time they have to complete it. It all boils down to organizational skills and time management. How well are you able to stay organized while using your time wisely over the course of the school year? You alone are in the position to know what kind of system will work best for your situation. How do you organize student grades, formative assessment data, homework assignments, discipline records, parent contact information, and so on?

Teachers often tell me that there's not enough time in the day for them to complete all their tasks. My response is always that they must closely examine how they use every single minute of their time. Chances are that many of those minutes are misused and wasted. Looking at your own day, how do you make the best use of your time? Have you examined your minutes closely? Are there any available minutes before or after school that you aren't currently putting to good use? Can you borrow minutes from your prep and lunch periods? You must continually ask yourself these questions to ensure that you are using all your time productively for the benefit of your students.

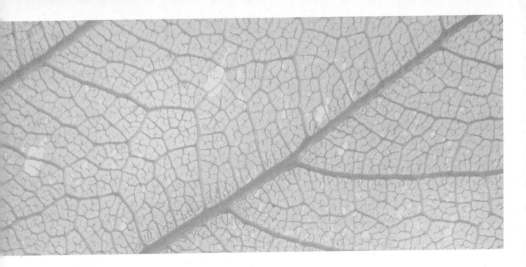

CHAPTER 9

Professional Development

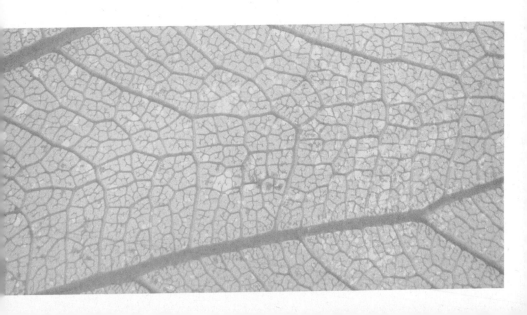

Q: To What Extent Does Professional Literature Enhance My Practice?

From my very first day as a classroom teacher, I felt it was imperative for me to always have some sort of professional literature in my possession to inform my daily practice. As a beginning teacher, I felt that I needed to learn something new every day—and 28 years later, I haven't changed a bit. The only difference is that now I can read articles and books on multiple devices.

In my workshops, I like to ask the assembled teachers and administrators to take their current professional reading materials out of their bags and wave them in the air so we can all see what everyone is reading. I strongly encourage teachers to put their own professional reading at the forefront of their practice and to challenge themselves to learn something new every single day.

What professional literature do you currently have in your possession? What are you currently reading? How much time per day are you able to devote to your professional reading? What is your area of focus? Do you select material to read that speaks to areas in which you'd like to improve? Your professional growth has to become an obsession for you. You have got to be at a point in your practice where you absolutely feel that you must grow professionally on a daily basis.

The best way to stay current in your field is to join a professional organization. There is an abundance of them for teachers, including the publisher of this book. There's really no excuse for you not to grow professionally given the plethora of available resources. It's just a matter of disciplining yourself and making the time.

I would also encourage you to write in addition to reading. Your insights can be a valuable source of professional development for your fellow teachers. Start a blog, submit proposals to professional journals, write that book that you've always wanted to write. You are bound to have something to say that can benefit others. Learn all you can and share what you learn with both your peers and the larger public.

Q: How Often Do I Seek Out My Own Professional Development?

Let's expand on the previous question and focus on your overall professional development beyond professional reading. How often do you seek out your own professional development? How do you determine which opportunities are best for you? How often do you attend conferences, seminars, institutes, workshops, and webinars? Have you been able to successfully apply what you've learned through professional development in your classroom?

Ensuring your professional growth is absolutely imperative. I meet hundreds of teachers every year who are at their wit's end with their students, and I always remind them that they are dealing with an entirely new breed of pupil. The students in classrooms today exist in a world that is vastly different from just 10 short years ago. How are you going to connect with these students? Are you armed with the required information? Are you attending professional development workshops that address how millennials learn in the classroom? Are you taking advantage of opportunities that enable you to meet their academic, social, and emotional needs? Your professional development cannot be confined to the workshops that your administrators or district arrange for you; you must proactively seek out any opportunities to learn and grow in your profession. Your students absolutely depend upon you doing so.

I strongly recommend looking into online professional learning networks (PLNs) as you seek out resources. The social media explosion has given educators options for professional learning that didn't exist a decade ago. The information that PLNs provide is endless and invaluable.

Q: In What Ways Do I Benefit from the Knowledge and Experiences of My Colleagues?

Far too often in schools, teachers are isolated in the small worlds of their classrooms. From early in the morning to the end of the day, they restrict themselves to direct contact with students and seldom interact with colleagues unless they're engaged in a professional learning community.

In my workshops, there's usually at least one brand-new teacher in the audience. I always encourage the veteran teachers to embrace their new colleagues—to tuck them under their wings as they navigate the challenges of their new experience. Most important, I encourage them to share their knowledge and experiences. I encourage them to make the new teachers feel comfortable and at home in their new surroundings and to provide them with all the support that they'll need for a productive start to the school year and to maintain that productivity thereafter. This type of mentoring is a critical component of every new teacher's professional growth.

In what ways are you able to benefit from your colleagues? Are you able to exchange ideas, information, and experiences with them? How often do you and your colleagues take the time to share experiences and learn from one another? Does the culture of your school lend itself to teachers engaging one another in these exchanges? Professional development is much more than books and seminars; it is also the sharing of ideas and experiences among colleagues.

Q: Am I Open to Accepting Constructive Feedback from My Colleagues and Administrators?

It is one thing to exchange information and ideas with colleagues; it is something entirely different to receive constructive feedback from them. Are you open to accepting such feedback? I believe that our interactions with colleagues are most productive when trust is strong enough to withstand honest criticism. What's key is being open to the feedback; this is a big part of the way we grow as teachers. When we can accept that we do not know it all and that others who have already traveled down the road we are on might have something to teach us, we put ourselves in positions to learn a lot more about our practice. Even if we don't entirely agree with the feedback we receive, openness to learning from colleagues is essential to our growth as teachers.

Q: Am I Willing to Act upon Suggestions for Improvement from My Colleagues?

Once you have accepted constructive feedback from fellow educators, the next step is to act upon it. Some of the strongest professional development we can engage in involves observing and coaching one another as we teach. There is so much we can learn in these scenarios that we could never learn in a workshop. Mutual trust is vital to these experiences and goes a long way toward ensuring that we actually act upon our colleagues' suggestions for improvement. Do you engage in coaching with your colleagues? When your colleagues give you feedback, do you trust that it is sound and act upon it?

CHAPTER 10

Parental Engagement

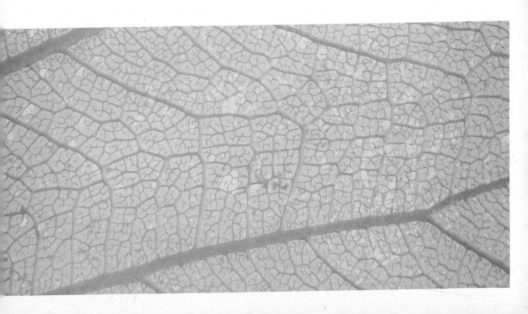

Q: How Strong and Productive Are My Relationships with My Students' Parents?

When I taught elementary school, my colleagues and I would brainstorm ways to collectively engage our students' parents. At one point it dawned on us that many of our students' younger parents, though well intentioned, simply didn't know how to assist their children academically at home. To address this, we decided to conduct our own parenting workshops. So, during each marking period, we offered workshops in which we provided parents with strategies and tips for facilitating their students' learning at home. These sessions were extremely powerful and enabled us to bond with parents, who were extremely appreciative of our efforts. The workshops weren't confined to academic issues—we addressed issues related to our students' social and emotional development as well.

In what ways are you intentionally building strong relationships with your students' parents? In what ways are you an asset to them? In what ways are your students benefiting from the relationships you have forged with their parents? Research has shown over the years that when parents are engaged, the likelihood of their children succeeding increases exponentially. It is your responsibility to consistently strive to build strong and productive relationships with your students' parents.

Q: How Often Do I Notify My Students' Parents About Their Children's Successes in My Classroom?

I vividly recall the days of calling parents at the start of each new school year. There were always a few who would exhibit hostility toward me, assuming I was calling to complain about something their children did in school. I was usually able to quickly allay their apprehension by letting them know that I was calling to introduce myself and tell them of the good things I had observed thus far.

Is calling your students' parents at the beginning of the year a part of your repertoire? How do these calls affect your students' behavior in the classroom? How do they affect your relationship with the parents?

During workshops, teachers often raise the issue of hostile parents. I tell these teachers that eliminating hostility is easy when we don't take it personally. When parents act in a hostile manner toward you, the best thing to do is to allow them to exhaust everything on their mind, including any insults they might wish to hurl your way. Do not argue back. Once the parents are finished speaking, cordially and calmly begin a conversation about the issue you wish to address while reassuring them that you understand their concern. I guarantee that this strategy will lead to a stronger relationship with your students' parents, but only if you subsequently work to sustain the relationship through ongoing dialogue.

When your relationships with your students' parents are strong and productive, your students are bound to feel more comfortable in the classroom and to do better academically. Work toward building those relationships with parents as close to the first day of school as possible and remember: introductions and compliments can go a very long way.

Q: Do My Students' Parents Have Access to Me?

When I became a high school principal, I decided that I wanted my students and their parents to have access to me whenever they needed to reach out, so I made my phone number available to everyone. Most of the time, those who contacted me did so via text message, which made it a fairly frictionless experience. Of course, I am well aware that this strategy isn't for everyone, but in my case it had a very positive effect on my relationships with my students' parents.

Do your students' parents have access to you? Do they know when they can reach you? Do you have set times during which parents can contact you? How do you make parents aware of the best times to call or visit? Parents who know that they have regular access to you will be much easier to work with over time than those who don't.

Q: Does the Input I Receive from My Students' Parents Matter to Me?

During my early years as a teacher, I initially and rather naively thought that somehow I had to be all-knowing. I very soon realized that this wasn't the case at all—my students' parents certainly knew their children better than I did and could teach me a tremendous amount about them. Input from parents matters a great deal, and allowing parents to express their ideas is an excellent way to engage them in their students' learning. Conversations are a two-way street, and parents who have something to say want to be heard. If you can provide them with the information they need about their children's academic, social, and emotional development while also remaining receptive to their input, you will always be a step ahead.

How do you go about soliciting input from your students' parents? How do you convince them that their ideas matter to you? How do you convince them that the role they play in the academic success of their children matters? Always keep the lines of communication with parents open and demonstrate to them that you think their input is invaluable for helping your students to thrive in the classroom.

Q: Have I Made Any Home Visits Lately?

I understand that home visits are not for everyone. Some teachers are just not going to feel comfortable sitting in the living room of their students' homes, particularly in challenging neighborhoods where the crime rate is high. But what an invaluable experience it can be for those who do venture out because it offers profound insights into the living conditions of students. When you visit students in disadvantaged neighborhoods, you are free to leave whenever you please, but the students do not have the same luxury. Appreciating this fact gives you a better understanding of how your students approach their time away at school, away from their home environments.

How comfortable are you with home visits? Do you see them as being relevant to your practice? If you make them, how often do you do so? What effect do home visits have on your expectations for your students? I cannot overemphasize the significance of home visits for those who are comfortable making them.

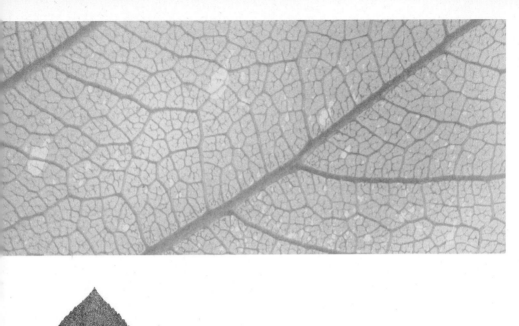

CONCLUSION

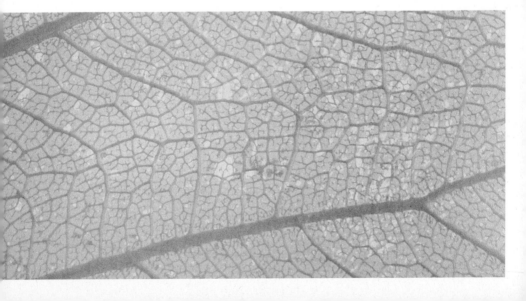

Over the years, countless teachers have disclosed to me that they feel as though they're burning out. Many of them tell me that they don't know how much longer they can go on teaching and that they feel defeated by the challenges they face. I'd like to take this opportunity to address the topic of teacher burnout specifically.

Each of us had a reason for entering the teaching profession. I would imagine that most of us can even remember precisely when we made the decision that teaching was what we wanted to do. At the time that you made the decision, I am sure that you felt that you were exactly what your future students needed. At that juncture, you went to work to make it happen. When you feel your energy start to wane—when you're discouraged, overwhelmed, or feeling defeated—try to connect with that younger version of yourself. Recall why you entered the profession in the first place and try never to lose sight of it. Never forget what you felt you were going to one day accomplish as a teacher. It is when we neglect to remember our initial impetus for becoming teachers that we lose our energy and end up burning out.

To maintain the high energy level that likely accompanies you at the start of every new school year, keep your self-reflection mirror handy at all times. Make sure that self-reflection, self-assessment, and self-adjustment are daily components of your practice. When you look into the mirror every morning, ask yourself the following three questions: Who am I? What am I about? What is my most recent evidence? If you do this, you will begin every day intentionally conscious of who you are, what your purpose is, and what you have accomplished in relation to both.

LIST OF 50 REFLECTIVE QUESTIONS

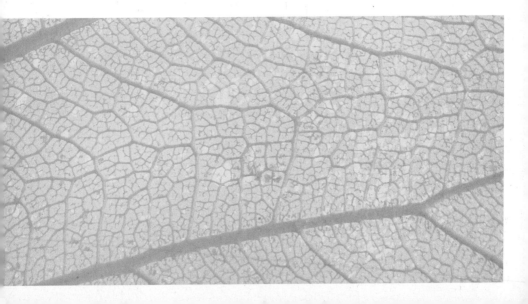

1. Are My Students at an Advantage *Because* I Am Their Teacher?

2. Why Do I Teach, Anyway?

3. How Badly Do I Want to See My Students Succeed?

4. Where Will My Students Be 10 Years from Now as a Result of Having Me as Their Teacher?

5. Do My Students See Me as an Example of Who and What They Can Become?

6. What Is My Signature Classroom Move?

7. Do I "Bring the Fire" into My Classroom Every Day?

8. Do I Believe That My Students Can Fly?

9. Have I Helped My Students to Put a Definition Next to Their Names?

10. How Do I Prevent My Students from Wearing Blindfolds in My Classroom?

11. Is My Classroom a "Bam!" Classroom?

12. What Is My Classroom's Way of Life?

13. What Is It About My Classroom That My Students Can't Wait to Come Back in the Morning?

14. Do I Teach *Math* or Do I Teach *Mathew*?

15. Is My Classroom's Brand Identity Conducive to Learning at the Highest Levels?

16. Do I Know My Students Beyond the Dismissal Bell?

17. Am I Intimidated by Any of My Students, Their Parents, or the Community in Which They Reside?

18. How Do My Students Perceive Me and My Treatment of Them?

19. To What Extent Am I Involved in My Students' Lives?

20. How Often Do My Students and I "Break Bread" Together?

21. How Do I Know Which Instructional Strategies Work Best with Each of My Students?

22. Who Are the True Stars of the Show in My Classroom?

23. How Do I Connect Learning Across the Content Areas?

24. Do I Take into Account That No Two of My Students Are Alike?

25. Does My Teaching Address the 21st Century Student?

26. Do I Consider My Students' Cultural Backgrounds When I Plan Instruction?

27. How Do I Infuse My Lessons with the History and Culture of My Students?

28. Do I Ensure That My Students Identify Culturally with the Lessons I Teach?

29. How Do I Demonstrate My Sensitivity to the Racial and Ethnic Diversity of My Students?

30. Am I Willing to Learn All That I Can About My Students' Cultures?

31. Do My Students Have the Option of Failing in My Classroom?

32. Do I Hold Myself Accountable for Student Failure?

33. Am I Willing to Accept Responsibility and Accountability for My Students' Successes *and* Failures?

34. Do I Reject Poverty as a Legitimate Excuse for Failure?

35. What Does My Mirror Say About My Effectiveness as a Teacher?

36. To What Extent Do I Prepare Beyond My Lesson Plans?

37. How Does Data Drive My Practice?

38. Have I Developed Expertise in My Content Area?

39. What Role Does Child Development Theory Play in My Overall Planning?

40. Am I Highly Organized as a Teacher?

41. To What Extent Does Professional Literature Enhance My Practice?

42. How Often Do I Seek Out My Own Professional Development?

43. In What Ways Do I Benefit from the Knowledge and Experiences of My Colleagues?

44. Am I Open to Accepting Constructive Feedback from My Colleagues and Administrators?

45. Am I Willing to Act upon Suggestions for Improvement from My Colleagues?

46. How Strong and Productive Are My Relationships with My Students' Parents?

47. How Often Do I Notify My Students' Parents About Their Children's Successes in My Classroom?

48. Do My Students' Parents Have Access to Me?

49. Does the Input I Receive from My Students' Parents Matter to Me?

50. Have I Made Any Home Visits Lately?

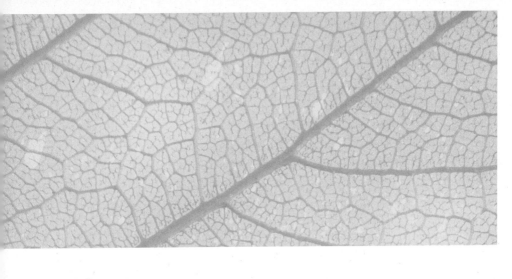

BIBLIOGRAPHY

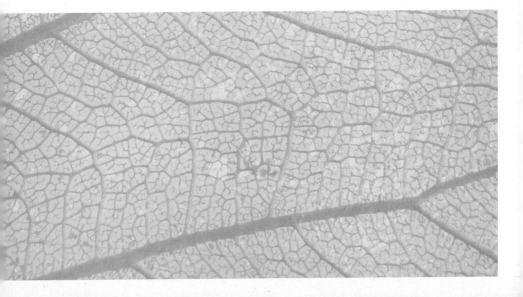

Akua, C. (2012). *Education for transformation.* Atlanta: Imani Enterprises.

Breaux, A., & Whitaker, T. (2015). *Seven simple secrets: What the best teachers know and do.* New York: Routledge.

Curwin, R. L. (2010). *Meeting students where they live: Motivation in urban schools.* Alexandria, VA: ASCD.

Gruenert, S., & Whitaker, T. (2015). *School culture rewired: How to define, assess, and transform it.* Alexandria, VA: ASCD.

Kafele, B. (2013). *Closing the attitude gap: How to fire up your students to strive for success.* Alexandria, VA: ASCD.

Mendler, A. (2014). *The resilient teacher: How do I stay positive and effective when dealing with difficult people and policies?* Alexandria, VA: ASCD.

Muhammad, A. (2009). *Transforming school culture: How to overcome staff division.* Bloomington, IN: Solution Tree.

Payne, R. (1996). *A framework for understanding poverty.* Highlands, TX: aha! Process, Inc.

Scruggs, T. (2014). *Be a parent champion: A guide to becoming a partner with your child's school.* Alameda, CA: Dirt Path Publishing.

Williams, K., & Hierck, T. (2015). *Starting a movement: Building culture from the inside out in professional learning communities.* Bloomington, IN: Solution Tree.

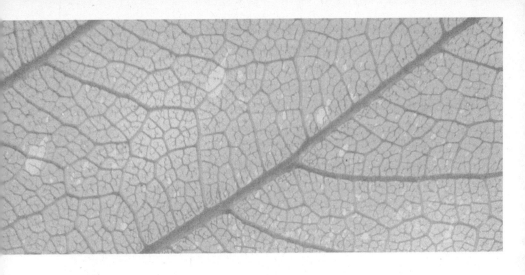

INDEX

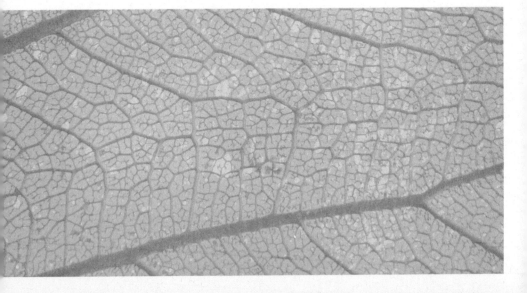

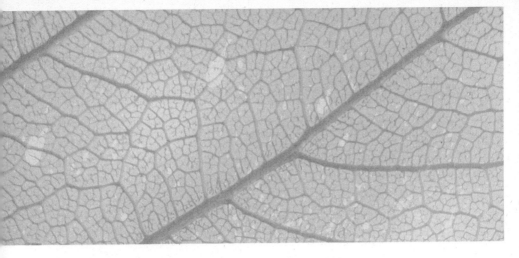

ABOUT THE AUTHOR

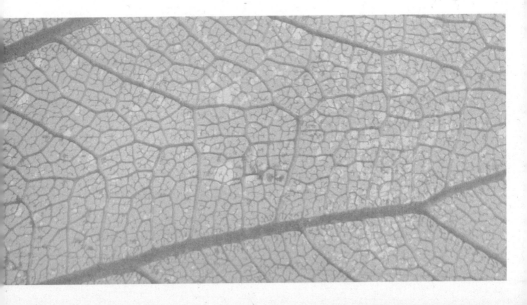

A highly regarded urban public school educator in New Jersey for nearly 30 years, Baruti K. Kafele has distinguished himself both as a classroom teacher and as a school principal. As an elementary school teacher in East Orange, New Jersey, he was selected as the East Orange School District and Essex County Public Schools' Teacher of the Year. As a principal, he led the transformation of four different schools, including Newark Tech, which went from being a low-performing school in need of improvement to being recognized by *U.S. News and World Report* as one of the best high schools in the United States.

Currently, Kafele is one of the most sought-after speakers on the topic of transforming the attitudes of at-risk student populations in North America. He is the author of seven books on this topic, including three ASCD best-sellers: *The Principal 50: Critical Leadership Questions for Inspiring Schoolwide Excellence, Closing the Attitude Gap: How to Fire Up Your Students to Strive for Success,* and *Motivating Black Males to Achieve in School and in Life.* He is also the recipient of more than 100 educational, professional, and community awards, including the National Alliance of Black School Educators Hall of Fame Award, the Milken National Educator Award, and the New Jersey Education Association Award for Excellence. Kafele can be reached via his website, www.principalkafele.com.

Related ASCD Resources: Inspiring Excellence in My Classroom

At the time of publication, the following ASCD resources were available (ASCD stock numbers appear in parentheses). For up-to-date information about ASCD resources, go to www.ascd.org. You can search the complete archives of *Educational Leadership* at http://www.ascd.org/el.

Print Products

The Inspired Teacher: How to Know One, Grow One, or Be One by Carol Frederick Steele (#108051)

Inspiring the Best in Students by Jonathan C. Erwin (#110006)

The Principal 50: Critical Leadership Questions for Inspiring Schoolwide Exellence by Baruti K. Kafele (#115050)

Qualities of Effective Teachers, 2nd Edition by James H. Stronge (#105156)

The Resilient Teacher: How do I stay positive and effective when dealing with difficult people and policies? (ASCD Arias) by Allen N. Mendler (#SF114077)

The Soul of Education: Helping Students Find Connection, Compassion, and Character at School by Rachael Kessler (#100045)

Teaching and Joy edited by Robert Sornson and James Scott (#196076)

Totally Positive Teaching: A Five-Stage Approach to Energizing Students and Teachers by Joseph Ciaccio (#104016)

Transformational Teaching in the Information Age: Making Why and How We Teach Relevant to Students by Thomas R. Rosebrough and Ralph G. Leverett (#110078)

The Twelve Touchstones of Good Teaching: A Checklist for Staying Focused Every Day by Bryan Goodwin and Elizabeth Ross Hubbell (#113009)

The Well-Balanced Teacher: How to Work Smarter and Stay Sane Inside the Classroom and Out by Mike Anderson (#111004)

When Teaching Gets Tough: Smart Ways to Reclaim Your Game by Allen N. Mendler (#112004)

For more information: send e-mail to member@ascd.org; call 1-800-933-2723 or 703-578-9600, press 2; send a fax to 703-575-5400; or write to Information Services, ASCD, 1703 N. Beauregard St., Alexandria, VA 22311-1714 USA.

THE WHOLE CHILD

The ASCD Whole Child approach is an effort to transition from a focus on narrowly defined academic achievement to one that promotes the long-term development and success of all children. Through this approach, ASCD supports educators, families, community members, and policymakers as they move from a vision about educating the whole child to sustainable, collaborative actions.

The Teacher 50: Critical Questions for Inspiring Classroom Excellence relates to the **engaged** and **supported** tenets.

*For more about the ASCD Whole Child approach, visit **www.ascd.org/wholechild**.*

WHOLE CHILD
TENETS

1 HEALTHY
Each student enters school healthy and learns about and practices a healthy lifestyle.

2 SAFE
Each student learns in an environment that is physically and emotionally safe for students and adults.

3 ENGAGED
Each student is actively engaged in learning and is connected to the school and broader community.

4 SUPPORTED
Each student has access to personalized learning and is supported by qualified, caring adults.

5 CHALLENGED
Each student is challenged academically and prepared for success in college or further study and for employment and participation in a global environment.